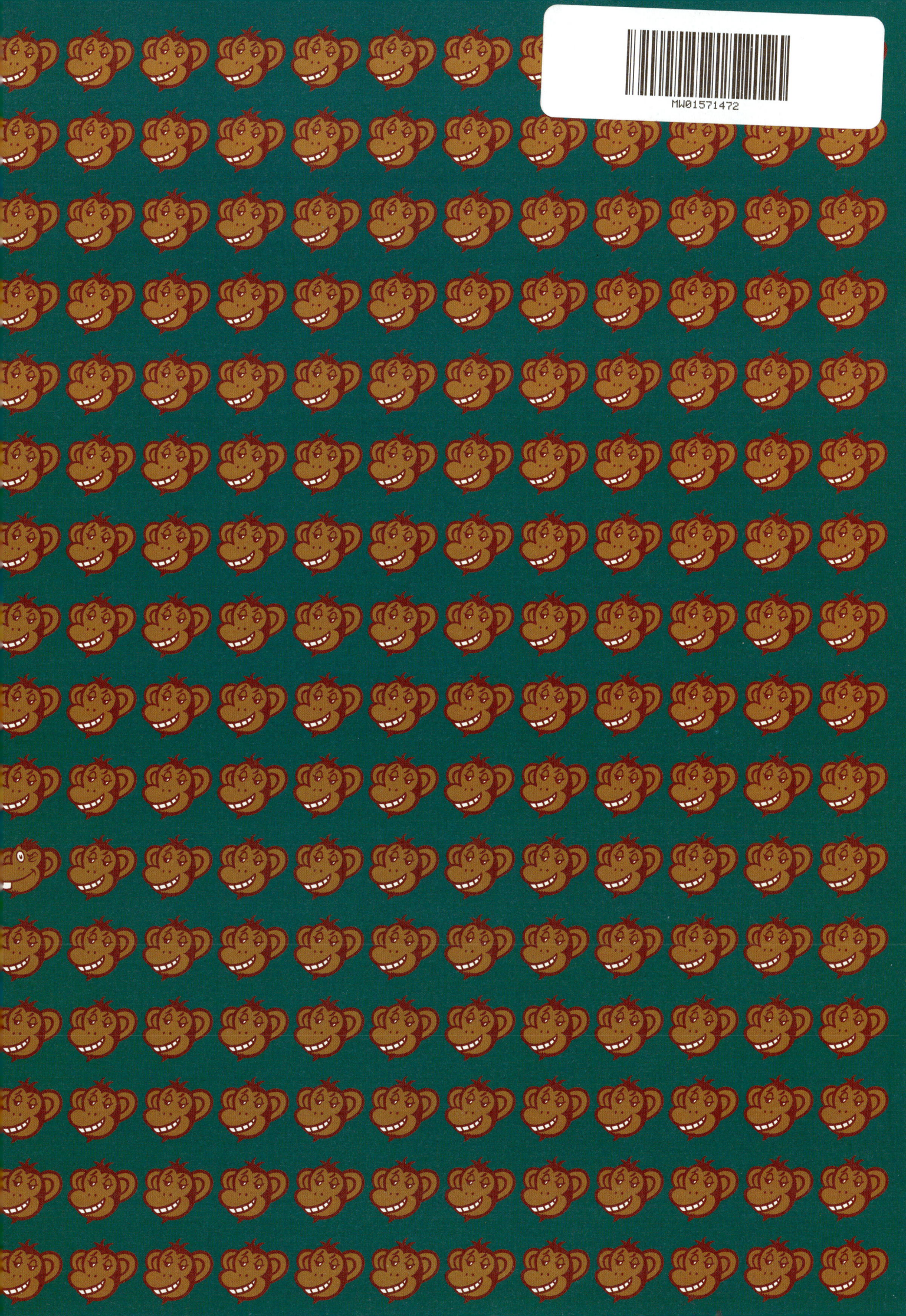

The Under Water Melon Man
© 1998 MONKEY BIZ LTD.

All songs & music
© 1998 MONKEY BIZ MUSIC LTD.

All rights reserved. No part of this book or recording may be used or reproduced in any form what-so-ever without written permission.

PUBLISHED BY
Monkey Biz Ltd, 81a Awa Road, Seatoun, Wellington, New Zealand.
www.monkeybiz.co.nz, E-mail monkeybiz@xtra.co.nz

TYPESET IN
OutWest, Sassoon Primary, ScalaSans, Bodoni Brush, Sackers Italian Script, Modula Rubbed, Tonnage, Leviathan, Suburban, Martin Grotesque, Tiki Palms, Tiki Holiday, Why not, Springtime, Bronzo, Huxley Vertical, Banque Gothic, Gill Regular, Gill Shadow, Kino, Fontesque, Fetish, Agfa Waddy 187, Champion Bantamweight, Mason Sans, Tiki Sands, Monkeybones, Helvetica Light, Regular, Black, Luvbug, Avian, Tiki Hut, Ziggy, Tabitha, Neo Bold, Sackers Square Gothic, Oz Brush Italic, Rosewood, Burnout, Badtype, Tiki Surf, Lower Eastside.

ISBN 0-9582010-0-5
Printed in China.

SPECIAL THANKS TO

Len Cheeseman
Type Direction

Hayden Doughty
Typography & Freehand magic

Saatchi & Saatchi Wellington
Generous support

Megalith
Generous support

Andy Sailsbury & Stephen Cicala
Photoshop magic

Guy Robinson & Marcel Trompe
Transparencies

Burton Silver & Melissa de Souza
Trade secrets

Jim Mitchell
Monkey Biz logo

Peter Dasent
Musical genius

Walter Donaldson & Edgar Leslie
Original idea for Imelda Blade

Geoff Blackwell
Never give up counselling

Neil & Sharon Finn
Hospitality and use of the Finn Home Studio

Arthur Baysting
Writing the very first rhyme

Tony Backhouse
Cheese fruit & vocal arrangements

All the Artists Musicians & Engineers

My Parents
For a great childhood

Shaan & Kaspar Flaws, Sally Zwartz & Tosca,
Frank & Coco Dasent
For patience, love & endless encouragement

DEDICATED TO MY AMAZING CHILDREN

Caitlin, Bonnie, Ginger, Venus, Buster & Kaspar

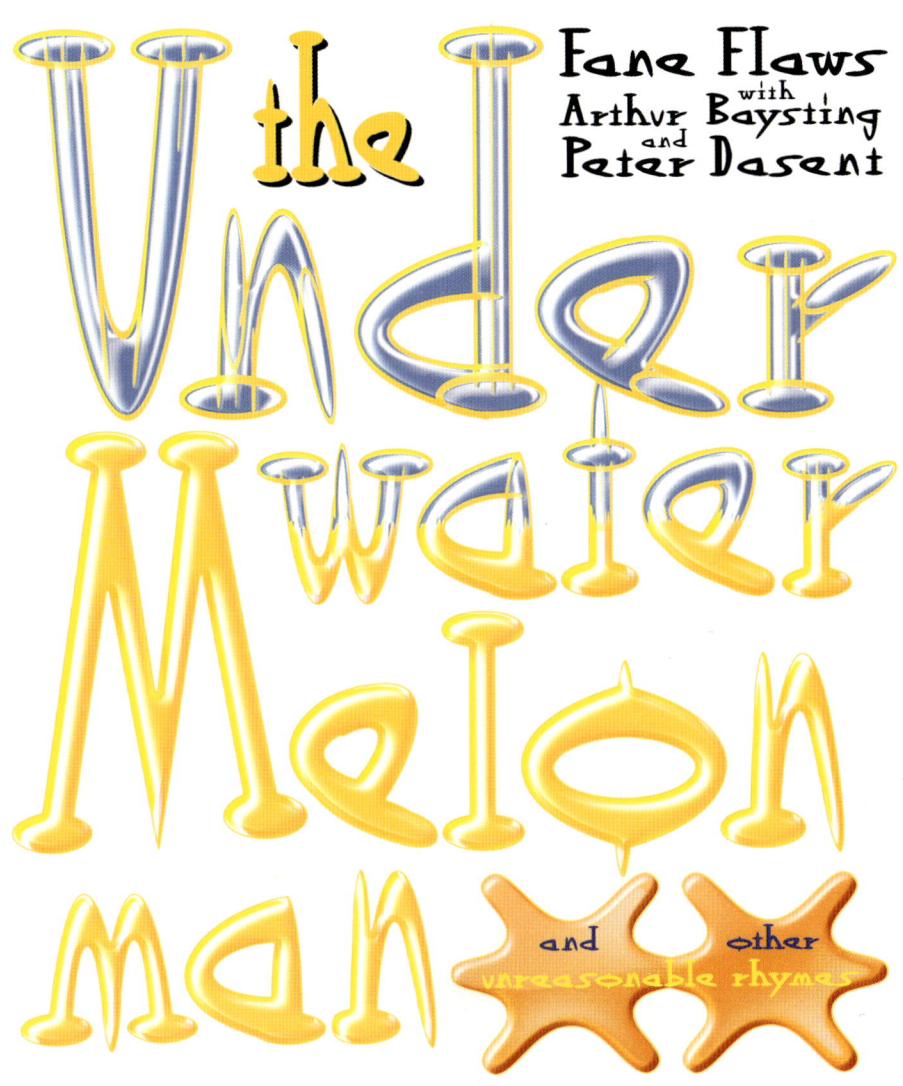

The Underwater Melon Man and other unreasonable rhymes

Fane Flaws with Arthur Baysting and Peter Dasent

Pictures – Fane Flaws
Music – 'Bend'
Type Direction – Len Cheeseman

the Underwater Melon man

He's really a most remarkable chap
An ingenious kind of a fella
He's invented the very first cactus-tap
And the wonderful desert umbrella.

Melon-Cauli Baby

Mr Wally Watermelon
And Miss Ollie Cauliflower
Took shelter in the tool shed
From a sudden summer shower
They tasted love's sweet blessings
'Neath a barrow dry and shady
And scandalised the garden
With their Melon-Cauli Baby.

The Girl with the Porcupine Coat

The girl with the porcupine coat
She's got the banker's goat
She sticks her bills onto the quills
And never spends a note.

THE MAN WITH THE CAST IRON BELLY

The man with the cast iron belly

Swallowed swords for a job on the telly

At night he'd relax

With a packet of tacks

And some razor blade trifle with jelly

His family and friends are aghast

As each breakfast may well be his last

Yes he's partial to snails

Only garnished with nails

In an omelette with staples and glass.

Neville The Enchanted Rug

For ten years on the parlour floor
It lay forlorn and cluttered
Until by chance one afternoon
The magic word was uttered
It shook itself and burst its tacks
And furniture aboard
Flew twice around the living room
And out the kitchen door.

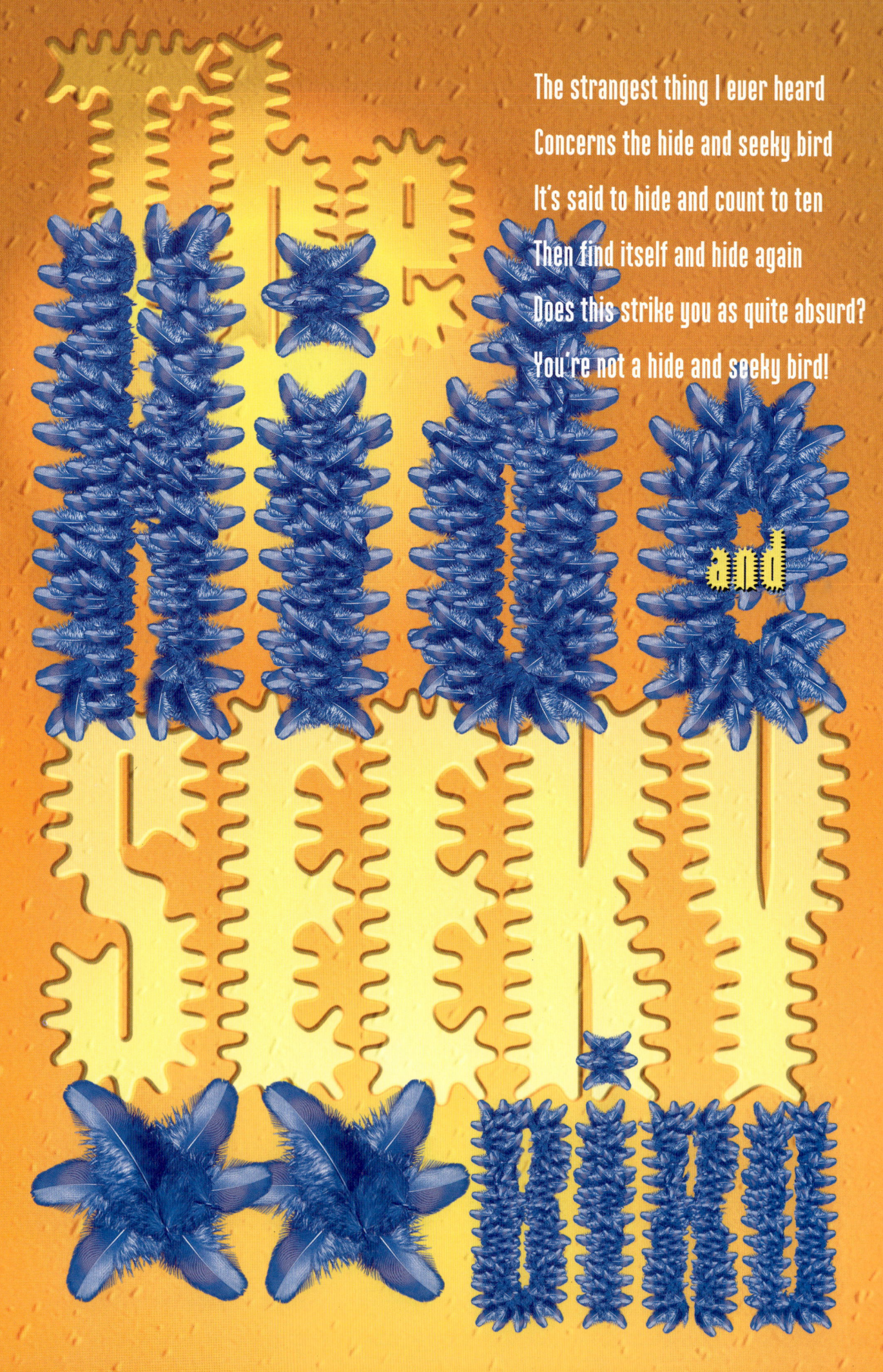

The strangest thing I ever heard
Concerns the hide and seeky bird
It's said to hide and count to ten
Then find itself and hide again
Does this strike you as quite absurd?
You're not a hide and seeky bird!

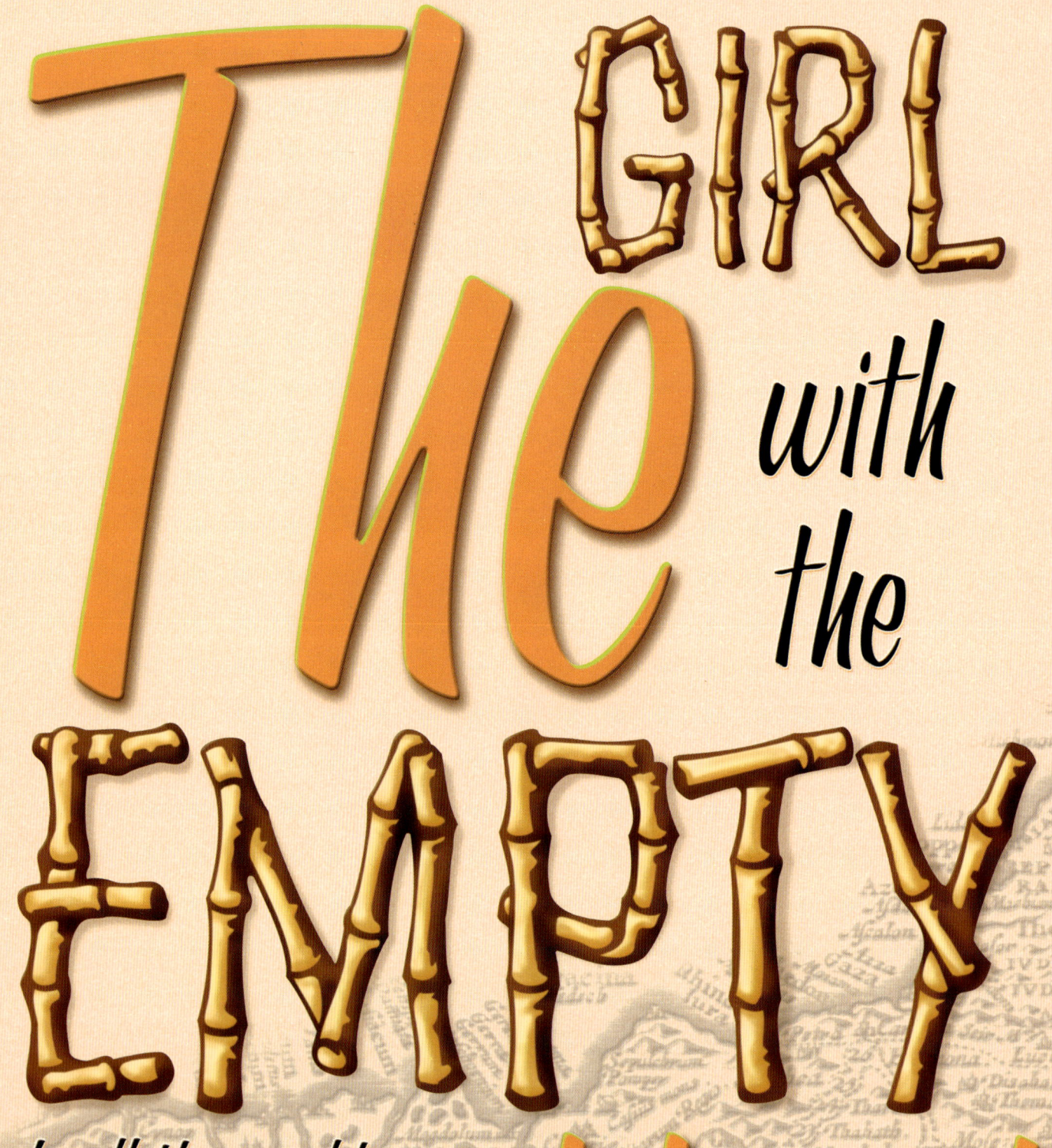

The Girl with the Empty Head

*In all the world
She hasn't a care —
She found a fortune
Buried in the sand
— And she left it there.*

The Trickster Conjurer

She's famous for her sleight of hand
And other nasty habits
She forces pigeons up her sleeves
And pulls hats......
Out of rabbits

She pays no heed to protocol
She does just what she pleases
One time she sawed a man in half
And left him......
In two pieces.

She's tamed a set of kitchen chairs
And woollen stockings, seven pairs
And even once a savage bunch
Of wild forget-me-nots
Big cats may be the common thing
But Miss Von B' goes in the ring
Unarmed..........
With five ferocious, live
Man-eating chamber pots.

Pottie Train

STRUCK 13 O'CLOCK

The colander accused the sieve of being full of holes, the pot informed the kettle it was black. The chips retraced their lineage back to the same potater. Then the tocks began a tickin'! And the ticks began to tock! The night the old Methuselah the kitchen taps began to run around the kitchen sink, and the oil told the butter it was fat. The cheeses all debated-"could the lesser hold the grater?"

Jemima Spride

Jemima Spride she loved to ride

Naked through the countryside

But what Jemima loved the best

Was bathing fully dressed.

KNIGHTS

We've heard about this damsel
the dragon wants to charm her
we've practised up for weeks on end
and now we're knights in armour
we've got the fastest horses
in case he wants to harry us
and when we kill the dragon
...... she's going to marry us.

THE FORGOTTEN  FORK

It was seven years ago today

The future looking bright

With a good job in the kitchen

And a cosy drawer at night

He was engaged to be married

To a lovely salad spoon

And they planned to raise some cutlery

In the upstairs dining room

When one crazy night Matilda

A hairy household pet

Knocked him down behind the cooker

And he hasn't been found yet.

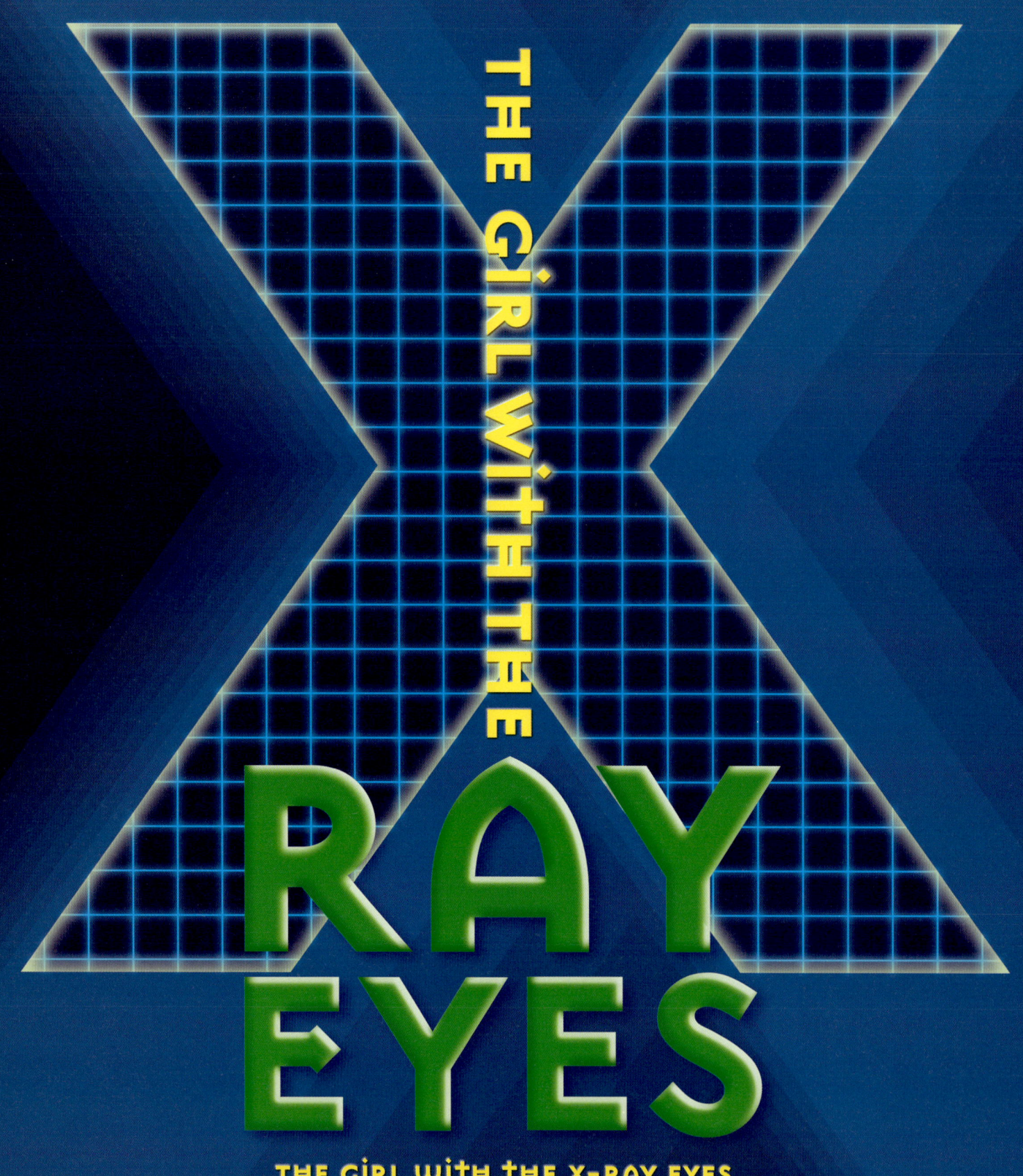

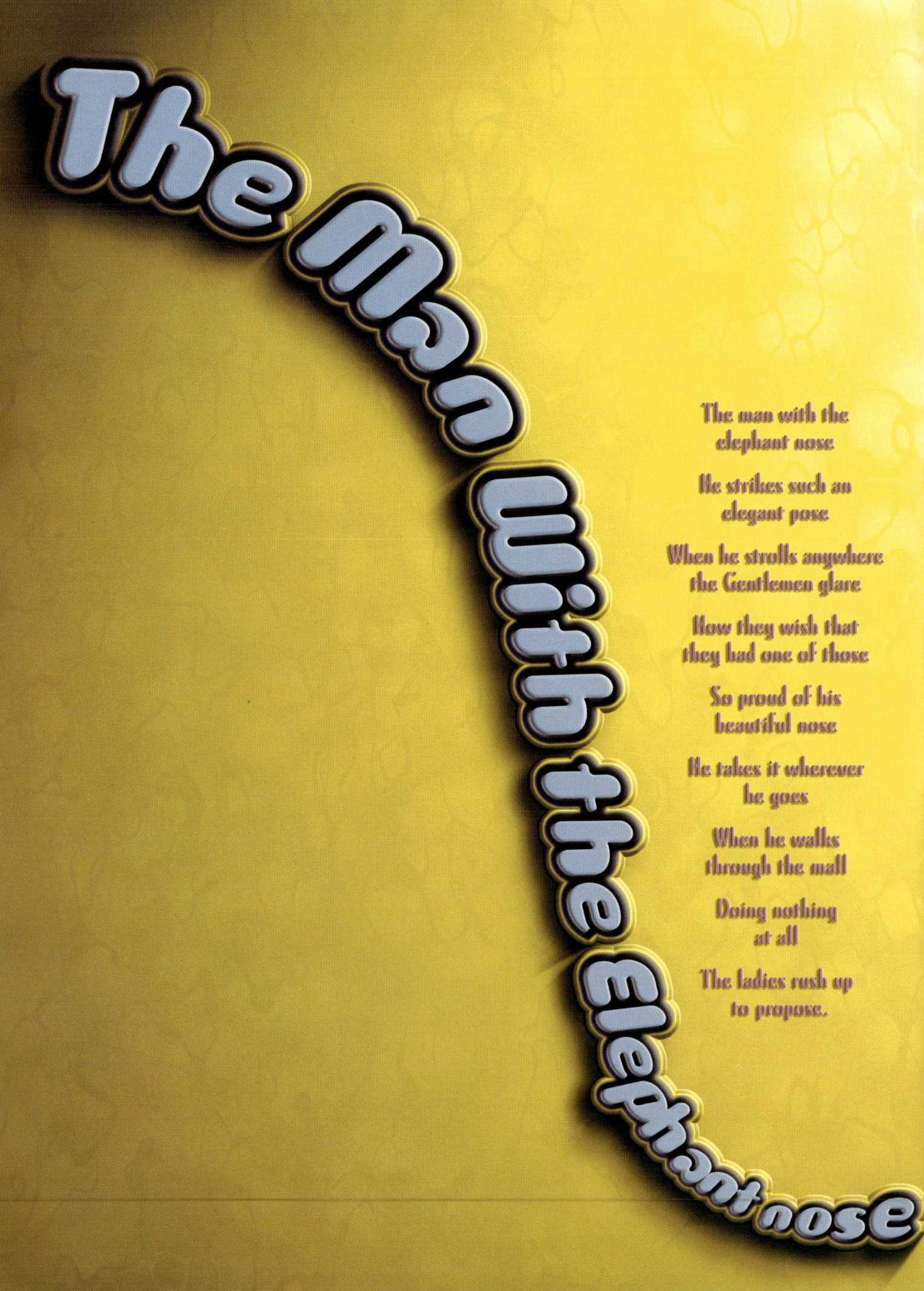

The Man with the Elephant nose

The man with the
elephant nose

He strikes such an
elegant pose

When he strolls anywhere
the Gentlemen glare

How they wish that
they had one of those

So proud of his
beautiful nose

He takes it wherever
he goes

When he walks
through the mall

Doing nothing
at all

The ladies rush up
to propose.

THE GIRL FROM GOD KNOWS WHERE

THERE WAS A GIRL FROM GODKNOWSWHERE

WHO WORE A MOP INSTEAD OF HAIR

AND FOR HER EYES, TWO BUTTERFLIES

HER EARS, PLAYING CARDS, ONE PAIR

HER NOSE WAS MADE OF MARMALADE

HER NECK A GLASS, HER FACE A SPADE

A RUSTY ZIP COMPOSED HER LIPS

HER HANDS AND FINGERS - FISH AND CHIPS

HER TORSO WAS A LETTER BOX

HER BREASTS TWO PLUGS, HER ARMS TWO SOCKS

HER ABDOMEN TWO SLIPPERS PINK

HER PELVIS AN OLD KITCHEN SINK

GATE POSTS FOR LEGS, DOOR KNOBS FOR KNEES

HER FEET AND TOES WERE LOCKS AND KEYS

SHE RAN OFF WITH A PORCUPINE

WHY? - YOUR GUESS IS AS GOOD AS MINE

'AND WHERE?' - THEY ASKED HER - 'WOULD SHE GO?'

HER ANSWER WAS..... 'GOD ONLY KNOWS'.

The Eccentric Instrumentalist

She takes her tuba out for walks
She wheels a little pram
She reads it bedtime stories
And feeds it toast and jam
She's really quite eccentric
The neighbours all agree
But she's happy with her instrument...
It keeps her company.

The Dog With The Saxophone

And the soulful melodious tone
He owes his fat lip
And peculiar grip
To the cat.....
With the slide trombone.

THE mysterious box

Why are we here?
What does life mean?
Where did it all begin?
The secrets of infinity
Lie hidden locked within.

The evil spell
That binds this world
Can now at last be broken
And every wrong put right
If only .... we could get it open!

THE PERFECT STRANGER

You find her on an empty beach

Or down some lonely lane

She seems somehow familiar

Yet you can't recall her name

You can't remember meeting

Or having seen her face

But the moment you're together

Not a breath is out of place...

So enjoy this perfect moment

When you look into her eyes

And you find you're in a heaven

And it comes as no surprise

But don't try to understand it

Or she'll fade herself away

To another perfect stranger

On another perfect day.

HE'S A DAREDEVIL TROUPER.
AN ACT WITH A TWIST
IF YOU VISIT THE CIRCUS
HE'S NOT TO BE MISSED
THE LIPS ARE SO RED
ON THE LADIES
HE'S KISSED

EL FLAMO

THE FIRE-EATING VENTRILOQUIST.

The Man Who Never Was

They found his shirt and trousers, his glasses, pipe and watch, his brolly, tie and bowler hat, his gloves, his shoes, his socks. But no one knows his whereabouts, or where he's from - because, No one has ever seen him...... He's the man who never was ....

She travels in the dream worlds

from her four-poster bed

she's friendly with an angel there

who was her uncle fred

she keeps a little diary

of everything that's said

she's got one thing upon her mind

and three eyes in her head

If you enjoyed 'The Underwatermelon Man and Other Unreasonable Rhymes' you may also enjoy 'The Boy With The Flaming Hair and Other Nefarious Notions'. Find out all about it and other great Monkey Biz titles by visiting www.monkeybiz.co.nz and while you're at it why not E-mail us on monkeybiz@xtra.co.nz

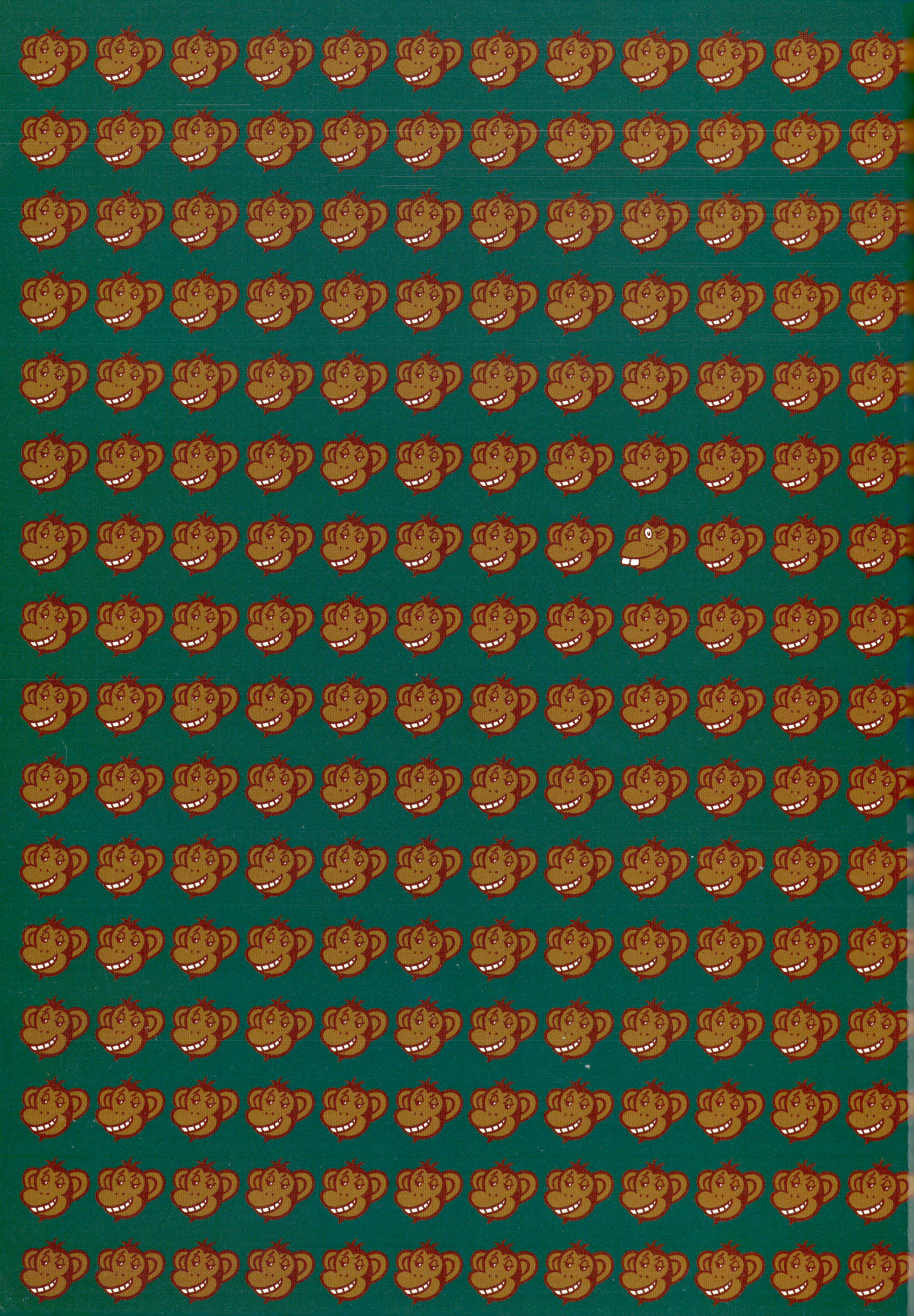